Relative Momentum:

AlbumBook

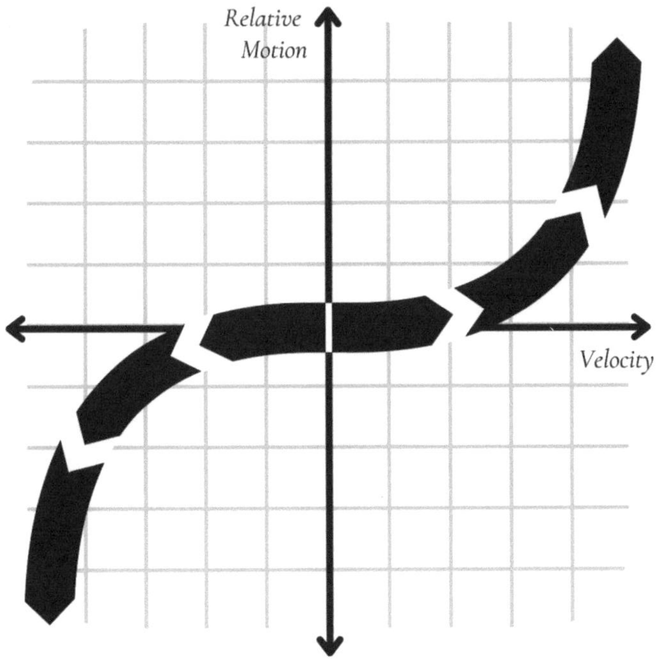

Jacob Conlan Shields

First Edition

These pages are to be used
by whomever,
for whatever.

Share your creative endeavor:
@Relative_Momentum
#RelativeMomentum

Concept Map

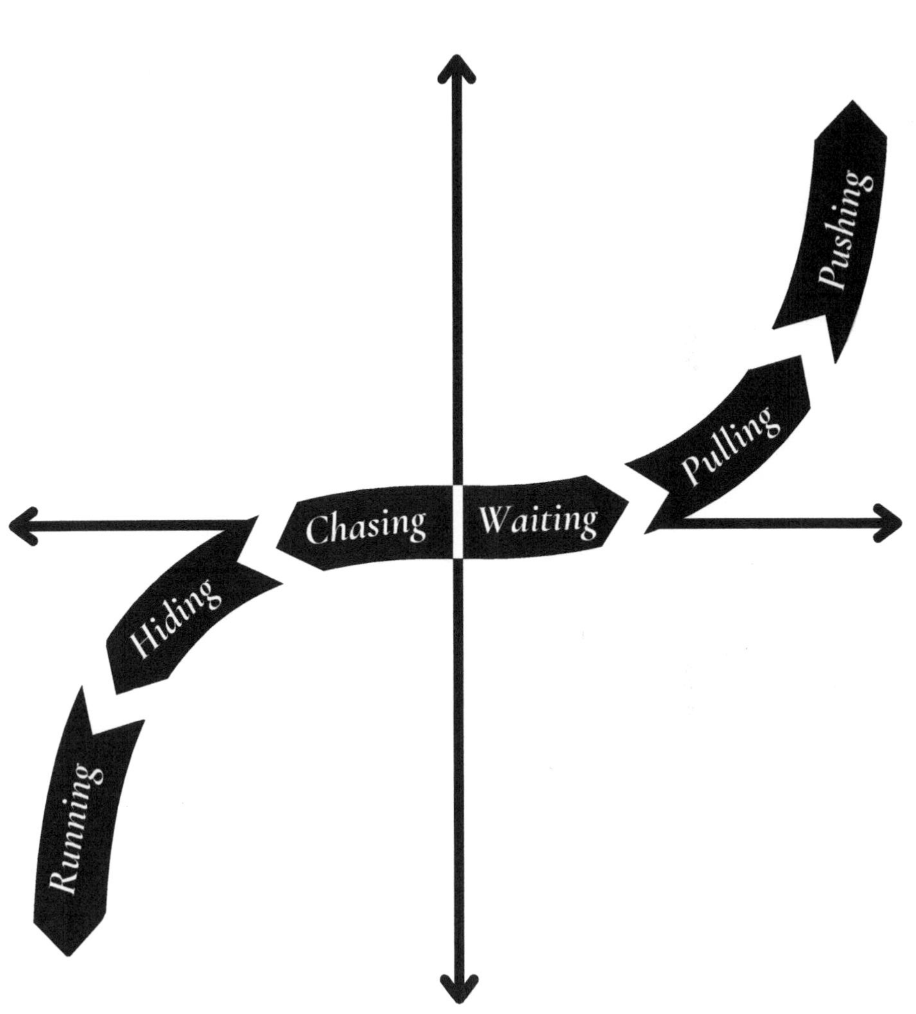

Contents:

Contents:

4) Waiting

5) Pulling

6) Pushing

1) Running

No Holds Barred

I'm on borrowed time
So it's all just house money.
She's out of my mind,
She just texted she loves me.
I wanted to want it
But wants just don't cut it.
My focus it jumped
Like I jump 'round the county.

Not All Who Wander Are Lost

Ain't lost I just wander,
Ain't searching I'm working
This path has its perks
but the picture ain't perfect
I try to live right
but the night it keeps lurking
The sticker price nice
But the interest ain't worth it

Art of Flight

I'm running from something.
Can't even describe it.
I've learned how to fight
But it's flight I'm designed for.
I know I don't hide
When push comes to violence.
But I keep up my stride
I'm lapping these milestones.

Hubris

Excuse
My lack of humility;
My ego is huge
But I temper it usually.
Worse for the wear
But emotions can't wear them.
You'll see that I care.
If I'm there it's apparent.

Sunk Cost Fallacy

I'ma run,
I'ma drift away blissfully.
If you want,
You can jump off this cliff with me.
I've run off so far.
Time heals over my scars.
This agua is aqua,
Come drink with me.

Vagabond

Don't know how long
This road carry's.
Full tank bags packed,
That's a pairing.
Next chapter,
Here's to new beginnings.
Cut my losses,
Keep my winnings.
Good tidings,
The tides are rising.
Tonight midnight launch,
Perfect timing.
Deep sea horizon,
Sails full, high winds.
Beam-reach, moonlighting,
North Star shining.

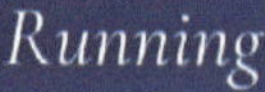

Round Trips

Been to hell and back,
I'm addicted to exploring.
Gave the devil daps,
Said I like your horns man.
Baby when the pain hits
I'ma just ignore it.
Running out of patience,
Need to press fast forward.

Full Tilt

I'm living in a frenzy
While I'm caught up in these notions.
Rooms tend to get all heavy
When my head unlocks and opens.
Don't know if I can help it
So it's time my ego owns it.
It's aces I was dealt
And now it's time to flip them over.

Tepid Tiger

Think I need
A Cus D'amato.
One to lead
That I could follow.
I'm a wild human being
And untreated
I'm a problem.
My needs, my greeds
Are seething
I've been fiending
For a while.
Intentions are mischievous
But believe I'll be
Role model.
I need someone to meet
My expectations,
They got higher.
I need someone to teach me
Who ain't preaching
To the choir.
Free but inefficiencies
Still keep me bottled.
My ceiling's got me reeling
But I'm scared to tear the throttle.

Everything's An Ashtray

I'm a runner, I'm a racer,
I don't ever owe no favors.
You want to meet up later?
I'll be gone to catch a plane or sumn'.
It takes too long explaining,
Best be on my way.
I'm running.
I'm a drifter, I'm a whisper.
I'll waver but won't whimper.
If I changed into a giver?
I bet I wouldn't stave off love.
Not interested in kickin' it.
I've got my ways.
I'm stubborn.

Perpetual Motion

I think my mind's contagious
And I fear these views are dangerous.
For me there's no complacent
So I'm on the go from place to place.
Sometimes I stop to wonder,
Am I saving souls or saving face?

Traveling Moonbeams

I'm a gypsy on a journey.
All I know now is divergence.
Don't leave the light on for me,
It ain't likely I'm returning.
Plus I'd be a different person
Since I stay updating versions.

2) Hiding

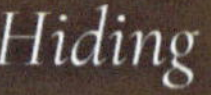

In Need Of A Thrill

What does it mean to live?
I know you can't leave when I sin
It's nothing to lose and nothing to win.
Tighten the noose up under my chin.
Bet you can't do it,
Means that you're human.
Nothing to prove, I'll never pretend.
Stuck in a loop, in sight it's no end.
Stuck in this loop, in sight it's no end.

Never Begin

Tip of my tongue,
Stuck at the fringe.
Damn sure can't run,
Step, get the spins.
Burst off in spurts
But my will gon' give in.
Lost I've got naught
So I jot with my pen.
Good times will come,
I'll grumble and ramble.
Look back and read this
Like damn dude you're scrambled.
You're gasping just breathe,
You're stuck in a panic.
Off kilter unmanaged,
This stress I keep packing.
Lacking the bandwidth,
No progress, no planning.
Depressed, then I'm manic.
I'm stressed, then I'm happy.
Unbalanced and frantic,
Afraid life will pass me.
The peak that I'm after,
Don't know if I'm tapped in.

Hiding

Stuck in this skin,
Shit let me linger.
Blood leaves my head,
Tingles my fingers.
Everest awaiting,
My feet feeling heavy.
Afraid of complacency,
That's where I'm headed.
Yeah that's where I'm headed
My lemons are juiced
But I'll send it
No begging or choosing,
I'm empty.
So tell me the truth,
What's it to live?
With nothing to lose
And nothing to win.
There's nothing to prove,
I'll never pretend.
So I'm trapped in this loop
I should never begin.

Hiding

Calm and Fear

Stimulation engaging,
I'm lacking the patience.
Life is a game, shit,
Depends on the framing.
Where is the top?
I doubt I'll make it.
Pathways are clogged,
My brain's feeling hazy.
At peace in the dark,
I'll reach for the stars,
Try hard I'm in pain,
Now I'm straining.
You can say that I'm vein
But I really feel ageless.
Time has betrayed me;
Impatiently waiting.

Hiding

There's nothing to chase.
I'm alright in the basement.
Get ready, replace me.
I'm gone so I'm fading.
My brush strokes are wavy.
See lines like I'm painting.
Wound up and unwinding;
Debate my mind
I keep fighting
My angel is calm
While my demon is frightened.
In mind now I'm gone
But at least I feel heightened.
No such thing as wrong
When you don't know what right is.

Topographical Delirium

Must have drifted off.
Can't say where or how.
I think I'm lost.
Now I'm spinning out.
I'll pay the cost,
Drain my account,
I'm on the ledge,
Drained, talk me down.

Coping Diversions

You sit back,
I'll write my raps.
Split my swisher,
Fill your glass.
If you lie sweetly
I'll look past.
Whatchu think?
Down with that?
It's cool with me
Stay where we're at.

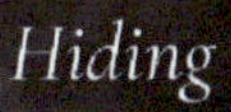

Time Dilation

I just broke down and cried;
It's my first time, I'll admit it.
Black it out I've been trying,
Now I'm high but remembering.
The years done flew by,
Shit, it felt like a second.
The clock it ticked slow,
I can't barely remember it.

Ignorance Treadmill

I ran loops 'til
My mind sore.
I had to let
My pride go.
Time to chew this
Humble pie, so
All I know is, I don't know shit.
Melancholy lost soul.
It's late they've
Prolly gone home.
Down to me,
I'm all alone and
All I know is, I don't know shit.
Where I'm going?
I don't know yet.
Hope this trip don't
Stay so hopeless.
Screwed myself, yep,
I'm the culprit.
All I know is, I don't know shit.
I break down, one-
Million pieces.
Blow my tree, since
That's my treatment.
Dopamine, I
Need to feel it.
I don't know shit, and that's my reason.

It's Hard to Die

Ain't hit my piff in 2 days now
I'm down, the high, I miss it.
Well shit, my tricks been running out.
Reality it sinks in.
I'm in and out of lucid thoughts.
My grips been known to slip and
Wane these days, I've lost my way,
Can I be changed? I'm trippin.
Can't give into the gimmicks.
Life's punch, won't dodge I'll chin it.
I'll just wing it, come out swinging.
What I'm smoking? What I'm drinking?
No plan, don't know what I'm thinking.
Can't undo shit, too far deep in.
Lady Macbeth, my hands, I'll clean them.
Hanging on threads, convinced I need them.
Every time I lose my mind know I get by,
Pick up the pieces, think I'm dreaming
I exhale deep, wait to breathe in.
Last I checked though, I'm still breathing,
I'm still breathing, I'm still breathing.
Last I checked though, I'm still breathing,
I'm still breathing.

"Non-Physical" Addiction

Let me hit this
Until it hits me, baby.
I gotta sip it,
To let my mind free, lately.
Don't think that I could quit it
I seem to have this need, maybe.
I want it when I want it,
Guess my greed plays in.

Least Resistance

Let's take the easy path.
No need unpack the facts.
Going nowhere, oh so fast.
Best ease our feet up off the gas.

Detached

I’m productive, I’m destructive;
Either way I’m thinking fuck it.
My mind is full of rubbish,
All these loops that I’ve been stuck in.
Lost for words my loved ones;
I'm far gone obviously.

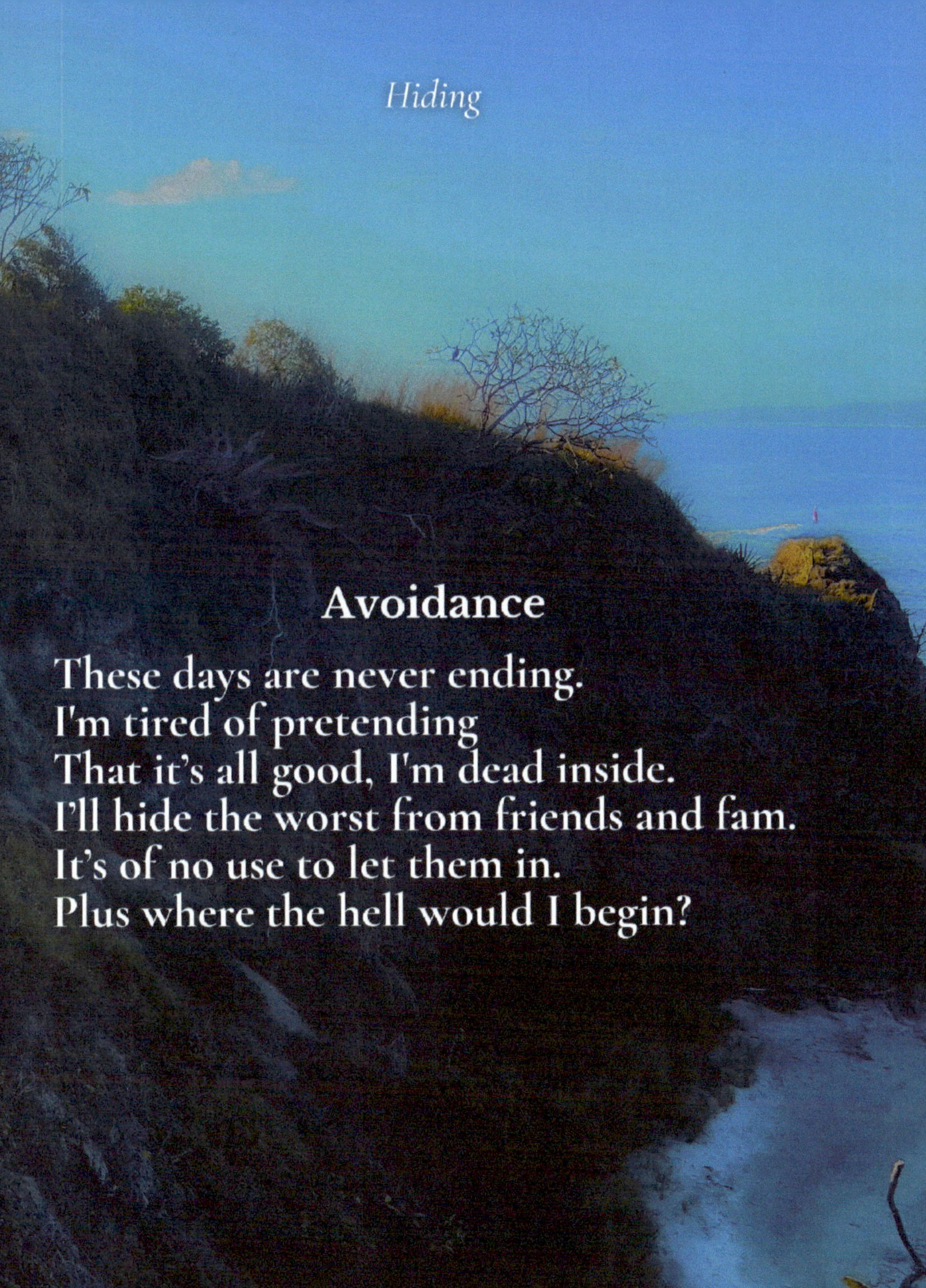

Avoidance

These days are never ending.
I'm tired of pretending
That it's all good, I'm dead inside.
I'll hide the worst from friends and fam.
It's of no use to let them in.
Plus where the hell would I begin?

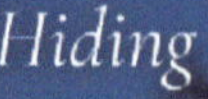

Ambivalent Chameleon

I keep shifting, I'm conflicted;
Multitudes, I'm contradictions.
I'm used to new beginnings truthfully,
'Scuse me if I'm cryptic.
Indecision, keep my distance
But at least here there's fresh air.
I've got nowhere to go
And a lifetime to get there.

Differentiation

Short term focus left me hopeless,
My past flocks me just like locusts.
Yeah it's karma, yeah I know it.
That's just life, no, yeah I chose it.

The Pits

I ain't jumped but I'm falling.
My demons are calling.
The future, I pause it.
Trapped in past, too much drama.
No 'shute a free fall.
Best watch out below.
No shute I'll free fall.
Best watch out belo-oh-ow.

3) *Chasing*

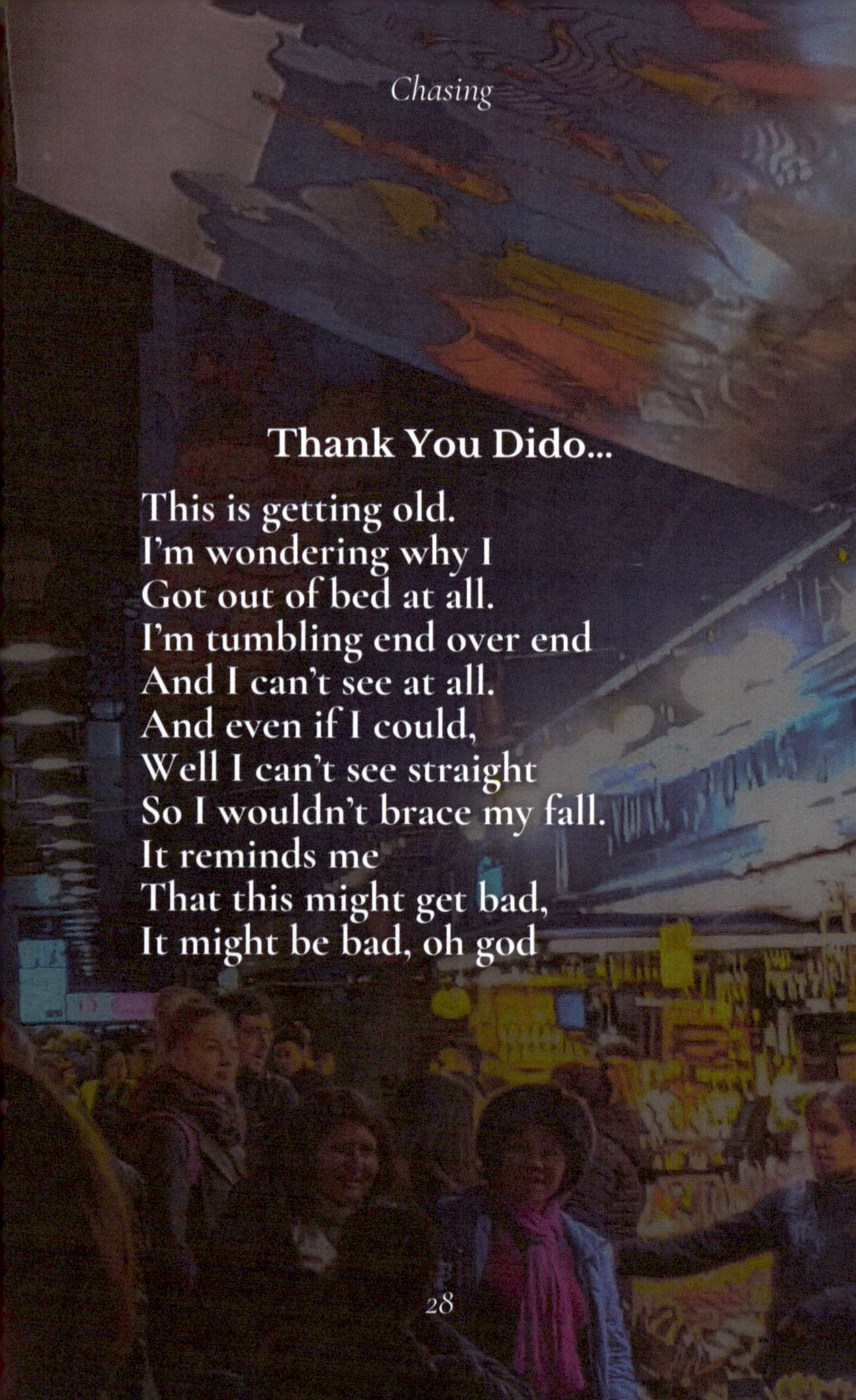

Thank You Dido...

This is getting old.
I'm wondering why I
Got out of bed at all.
I'm tumbling end over end
And I can't see at all.
And even if I could,
Well I can't see straight
So I wouldn't brace my fall.
It reminds me
That this might get bad,
It might be bad, oh god

Hell-Bent Chihuahua

Give me a sec, I'm breathless.
I chased my tail, I'm restless.
When it comes to risk I'm reckless.
I find limits when I test them.
Failures, don't regret them.
I don't let them take me over.
I'm a soldier, I keep pressing.
I can't stress on little shit
Since my big questions
Need attention.

Chasing

History Repeats

Another time, another place,
Another dime stood up a date.
I crashed another car,
There goes another bumper plate.
Look my eyes, they're red I'm high;
I won't disguise my mental state.
Well maybe I'm just wasting
All this time while I say
I'm dream chasing.
Ankle breaking,
Juking out the usuals.
On the fly creating,
Watch me doodle
When I'm zooted.
This ganja gets me lucid
Almost like a tab of lucy.
Brain cells fire in unison
All the neurons I'm recruiting.
I'm daily dose mushrooming,
2 on Tuesday and I'm grooving.
In tune feeling smooth,
I stay cruising through my routine.
These rules all seem so useless,
Tell me, ain't them suitses clueless?
No idea what they're doing,
Tell me, ain't them suitses stupid?

And I know absolutely,
I'm picking, babe I'm choosing.
Ungrateful fool, impatient dude,
A blind eye to the future.
I hate to lose, I'll pay my dues,
I find the pain is soothing.
I'm breaking loops, and chasing truth,
What it means to be a human?
When I'm rhyming I can't try,
It just happens, I can't do it
I find these lines intrusive
But they're sweet, they glide like sucre.
Deep they ooze in juices,
I'm just here for distribution.
A vessel for this music,
I just try to not dilute it.
I'm high like helicopters,
All my joints are fat and juicy.
I'm smoking like I'm Rasta,
And my life feels like a movie.
I think I'm living proper
But I feel I'm disillusioned
My mind spins like a washer
But it's chopped up like a smoothie.

Well that's my thoughts but who gives?
I'm gravy, call me poutine.
I'm made of rock like Bruce Lee
And I break the box like Houdine.
So make some room, go scoot your booty.
Got a clue, it's coming to me.
Got a map, I sketched it loosely
On a napkin, my solution.

Unstoppable Force

I'm jobless, she's topless,
No obstacles stopping me.
Darling, I'm sorry,
It's better off probably.
Can't share your sentiment,
Sorry for ending it.
It's coming my day, in the end,
Yeah, it's got to be.

Action Oriented

These missions await
And I'll chase, and I'll chase,
But I know where my place is,
I'll return if you'll take me.
It's harsher the truth,
When there's something to lose,
You're my favorite so I'd hate if
I cause rumination.

Wanderlust

Well time keeps on ticking,
I belong in these transitions,
I don't sit still.
If I'm here well then I'm in it,
Or I'm off into the distance,
There's no middle.
I love the ways you're different,
And really we've been clicking,
Life's a riddle.
Whatever comes with it I'm risking,
I feel bad for my decisions,
Just a little.

Aimless Pursuit

Now I'm chase, chase, chasing.
What's my time?
I gotta shave it.
What's the rush?
I can't explain it.
Is it to or from I'm racing?

Lucky 3's

It's been a goddamn while
Since I thought about these topics.
You're stirring something I forgot.
Please bring it up, don't drop it.
Attention lacking, I'm distracted,
Escaping, staying locked in.
I'm chasing babe, I'm late OK,
I don't mean to be obnoxious.
It's lucky 3's, have trust in me,
I know you know you're worth it.
I'm slow but I be learning,
Just 1 way to know for certain.
I'm old enough to notice
That there's always space to focus.
There's always space to grow this.
At least that's what my hope is.

Slippery Slope

All this time passed,
I've been dying.
Spiraling down,
I've been sliding.
Pick up speed,
Guts butterflying.
Truth is that I
Kind of like it.

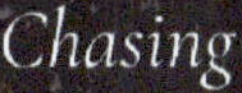

Un-Charmed

Sacrificed surprise in life
To see behind the curtain.
I've gone despite bright warning signs.
No wrong, no right, just light behind.
These gears keep turning furious,
I've built up too much endurance.

Turkish Royals

Like a ghost, think I'm haunted.
I'll get up then fall quick.
I'll smoke 'til I'm coughing
Then I blame exhaustion.
I'm dizzy, I'm nauseous,
I'm busy but jobless.
Keep trudging, don't call quits,
The wind I throw caution.

Stories of Pain

I could fill this book up
With stories of pain.
It wouldn't change
Your frame of mind.
I know that it's lame
But fuck it I'll try.
I might go insane
But fuck it I'll try.

Hustling Backwards

I'm chasing time is wasting.
Another lifetime maybe.
No rest, no break for patience,
Another lifetime maybe.

4) *Waiting*

Innocently Lurking

Don't be frightened,
Know I've got you.
Clear winds on horizon.
Here's my chips now I'm in.
Do your thing won't stop you.
Like to watch you when you're vibing.
Find peace within the silence,
I'll be patient, wait good timing.

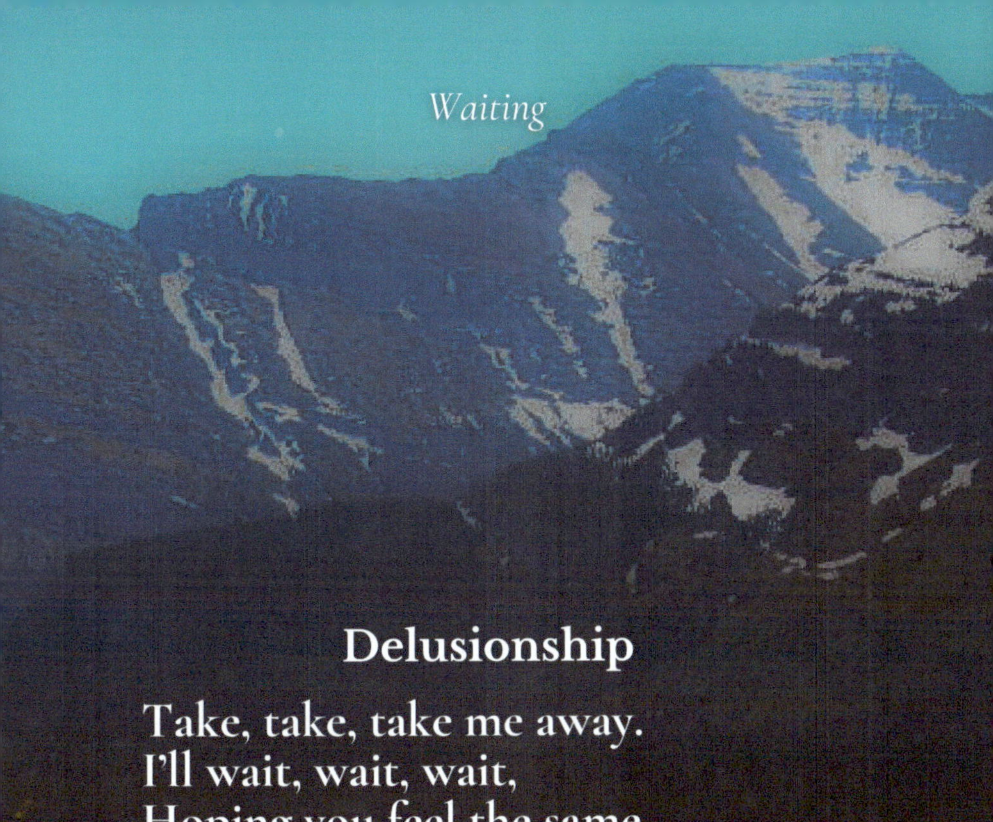

Delusionship

Take, take, take me away.
I'll wait, wait, wait,
Hoping you feel the same.
Shake, shake, shake, me awake.
Can't even say lately
If this dream world is fake.

Cognitive Dissonance

Her family is distant,
They mind their own business.
She don't keep tabs much
Because they have differences.
Decisions made,
She didn't care if they liked them
And now her eyes glazed,
She numbs pain with them Vicodins.
Or maybe it's perkeys.
I can't say for certain.
She just said she's high
Since it helps when she's hurting.
She's living estranged
And alienated
But designer bracelets
Keep her from complaining.
She's in her lane
And her Tesla can change it.
There's freedom to gain
And her life's what she makes it.
She doesn't seem strained,
She doesn't need saving.
Her walls barricaded,
Steel fortification.
She longs for home
But she can't replace it,
All she chases,
Good vibrations.

Dysphoria

Jack and coke with and a bean
To the dome, to the kidneys.
Her pregame routine
Just to start off the evening.
Out of town for next weekend
So this one has meaning.
Sick of this place so she's leaving,
Somewhere warmer this season.
She's headed to south beach,
It's work and vacation.
She says it gets rowdy,
With yachts and champagning.

The Space Between

Transnationalizing her relationships.
She's acting through life
And she's making her tips.
She's sitting right there
And staring right through me.
I am transparent,
She sees she can’t use me.

Low Doper

She's a low doper
At least so she claims.
And it's hard to stay sober,
Once thresholds get raised.
Piece a soul for a Rover,
That's a decent exchange.
But she don't know bout romance,
And love's out of range.

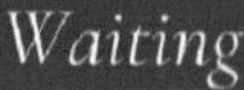

Iminent

I can't steer this ship we're veering.
Going nowhere, are we near yet?
Storms approaching, dear I hear it,
I can sense it, do you fear it?

Anchoring

Ain't no one flawless.
Wait out the darkness.

Traction

Came up slow and easy.
Life got fast, somehow I keeped up.
Still here though, no rhyme or reason;
Didn’t know so much, can't believe it.
Made the process pure for sure.
Now I'm jumping, bound and leaping.
Store the memories I'm keeping,
I was quiet, now I'm singing.

Empty Gravity

What should I say
When I can say anything?
What would I change
If I could change anything?
Where would I lay
If I could lay anywhere?
It's hard to refrain
When I want to chase everything.
What should I make?
In the end I break everything.
What's it to live
And feel the same everyday?
What I would give
To never take anything.

Lifetimes to Spare

In another lifetime
We'll line up at the right time.
This path I chose is overgrown,
It's dark like it's the nighttime.
You're right, stay on your tight line,
May your heart hold hope unlike mine.

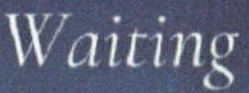

Outside Looking In

Religion, sheesh.
I never really got it.
Truly don't see
How y'all adopt it.
Think it's their place
To tap into your pockets
So you can die and go to space
Without a goddamn rocket?

Waiting On Forever

Everybody
Follows the same lines.
In the name of God
They don't stop to ask why.
They say that miserable
And their face reads abysmal.
Seeking relief
Not in inner peace
But in the exterior.
Living in fear
It appears
That they're feeling inferior.
They walk the walk
And talk the talk
But their heart is lost
And their spirit is locked.
Alright, I'll stop,
Won't continue to harp.
I too walk the walk
And too talk the talk
So my role probably
Is a part of the flock.

Either Way

If there's a God
Then God has got him.
Whether or not,
His body's rotting.
His life is lost
But not forgotten.
Pills, they kill,
Fent, oxytocin.

On Despondency

Seen plenty
Go weak
In the knees.
Victims,
They plead,
They say please.
Don't know what they seek,
They just need some relief.
They doubt their release
But belief is the key.

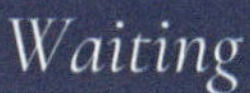

Full Commit

I think about it a lot.
Could my brain decide
To commit true suicide
And force my heart stop
With no noose and no knot?

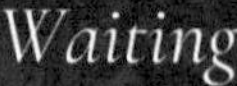

Totaled Ford

I crashed a car again, geez.
So now I'm pinching pennies,
But at least my tank was empty.

Street Poet

I’m paycheck to paycheck.
I can't pay so rain check.
I hate stress, I can't rest,
I live more and make less.

5) Pulling

Brother

Yo lil bro,
I'm lowkey geeking.
Seen your demons,
They keep scheming.
Seen you slipping,
You've been sipping.
I keep wishing
You could kick it.
When you're with it,
Bro, you're with it.
But Christmas,
You almost missed it.
We both had it
And we pissed it.
I just wish it
Wasn't so risky.
Count your gulps,
At least 2 digits.
Seen you fidget
When you’re itching.
Life is boundless,
Death is rigid.
Don't take shortcuts
To the finish.

Posterior Activation

I hope that time
Will heal ya.
I can see that
You need rehab.
Hope this re-collapse
Gon' be ya last.
Shake ya demons
Free at last.
But I don't know,
It ain't no telling.
Cant see the future,
I'm left guessing.
Ignorance might be a blessing.
For the time being though,
I'm left stressing.

More Than A Game

The want, I know you have it.
Your life, don't go and trash it.
Get your feet and reestablish.
Tap in, not out, go ahead grab it.
Know you can't stay the same,
Need to change, can't just end it.
This shits more than a game
When you face consequences.

Fam Shit

I dropped you off
And called your mom up.
Told her my past
Too was haunted.
Told her that
The way I saw it,
Believed you're good
But couldn't promise.
Needed her to know
That I felt sorry.
Not my fault,
Still feel responsible.
She's been through it,
Told her I got it.
We want the best,
Pray you can drop it.

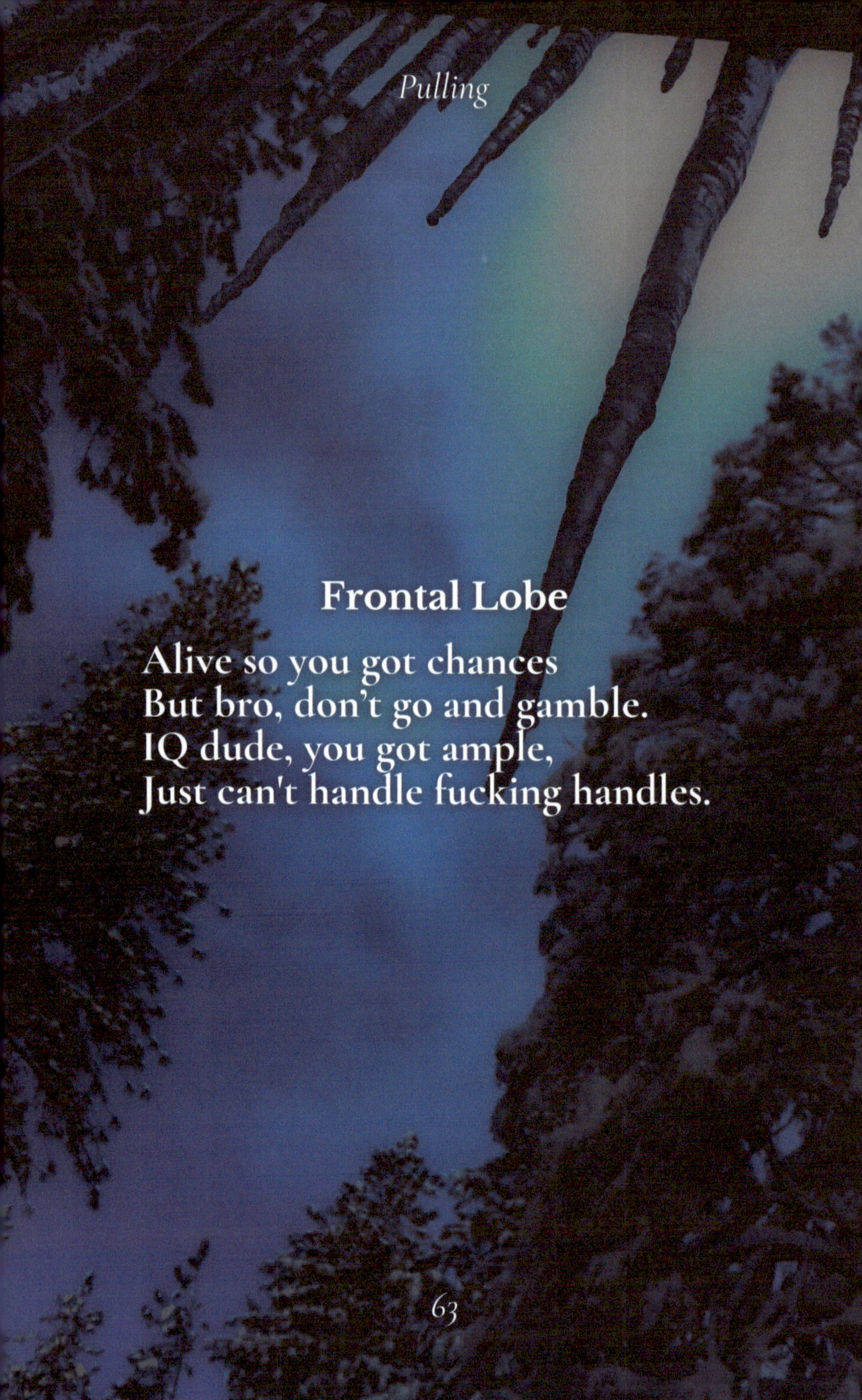

Frontal Lobe

Alive so you got chances
But bro, don't go and gamble.
IQ dude, you got ample,
Just can't handle fucking handles.

Class Clowning

Life used to be so easy.
We were both obnoxious geeks then.
Back of class, consistent seating,
Interrupting, speaking freely.
Too smart, answers, didn't need them.
April fools, we're pranking teachers.
Too cool for school, didn’t think we’d need it
But man I wish those days could be it.

Chutes and Ladders

I've got your back,
No broken trust.
Don't make me live
For both of us.
Don't trip on me,
I'm holding up.
Don’t go and die,
Not old enough.
Go get your help
And soak it up.
Don't play the game
To lose it.
Climb ladders
Then you're chuting;
Cruise up the board,
Don't fold it up.

Free Your Cool

It is what it is,
Couldn't be any different.
We done grown up,
Confront afflictions.
Made peace with mine
But you're still trippin.
You missed the goal,
At least you're kicking.
Couldn't live so vivid
With inhibition.
Change you outlet
Or you'll keep tripping
Alcohol is unforgiving,
Don't notch it down,
Fuck, just grow bigger.

Fear Setting

I'm afra-fra-fraid
Of the light I like it shady.
All my nights been troubled lately;
At times I'm lost in maybe's.
I've been face, face, facing
All my fears, I've been embracing
All these uncomfortable spaces
Which makes me feel audacious.

Crossroads

You always wear that face.
Day after day it never changes.
Pride I'll swallow, I won't rage.
I'll turn the page and hope you follow.

Fat-Tail Focused

I'll put myself first
And it hurts me if I hurt you
But I've learned on our journey
If there's will we can work through.
Uncertainty, it hangs,
My heart pangs and I'll thank you.
My plans can be a handful
But my gut has always rang true.

Un-Spiraling

Found some passions,
Call it meaning.
Took so long,
Damn I was pleading.
Wasn't easy
But no grievance.
Take my spirit
Over green bills.
Wealth in mind,
Wealth in soul.
As I grow old,
Hope those my goals.
I can't write,
So I was told.
This shit ain't school,
I'm schooling phonies.
Fam around
When I get lonely.
Keep it lowkey,
Watch the homies.
Keep an eye out,
Those who know me,
Not 'bout saying,
All 'bout showing.

Whittling Away

I'll go with the grain
Of the grooves that I've greased
Less the graves of my egos I've slain.
I'll show you cuz, babe,
I know it's no use
To believe that I'm bound to refrain.

Warp and Weft

The times drawing near
When I'll feel out my fears,
I've been broken.
I hope that it's clear
I ain't fleeing from here
But I'm going.
It kills me to leave
And I hope that you see
You're my woman.
If you can't go be free
But I hope that we weave
'Til we're woven.

6) Pushing

Integration

Ignore the fucking details,
Next step forward, ain't no cheat codes.
My bank accounts at zero
And I just ran out of pre-rolls.
Ain't waiting on no hero
Since I've set it straight before.
I hate to brace to face my face
To see what the mirror shows.

Immovable Object

I'm trying to try,
I'm dying inside.
Truth is I'm losing,
My loose ends untied.
I'm soft,
Life chews me up toothless
And spits me out clueless.
Self-worth is useless,
As too is my drive.

Scars to Show

Give me a second.
No a minute,
No a year.
Hoping I catch up
But I've got
No idea.
I am spent
But I keep spending.
Leaving dents,
The blemishes blend in.

Nonlinearity

It was never the plan
To stay crashing.
Now I'm flabbergasted,
All mixed and no matching.
No hand I can manage,
I handle time passage
But add up the damage.
A sailor no captain,
Feel captive no passion,
I'll toke on this cabbage,
And hope it relaxes.
Down then I'm up,
That's just how it happens.
Drown out the sounds
My loud stereo blasting.

Knockoff Ice

If I glitter, I'm faking,
I'm plated, not golden.
I'm hiding my shame since
At core I feel broken.
Don't peep cards when I'm folding,
The options my only,
Hate watching doors closing,
Don't see it don't notice,
'Least that's what the goal is.

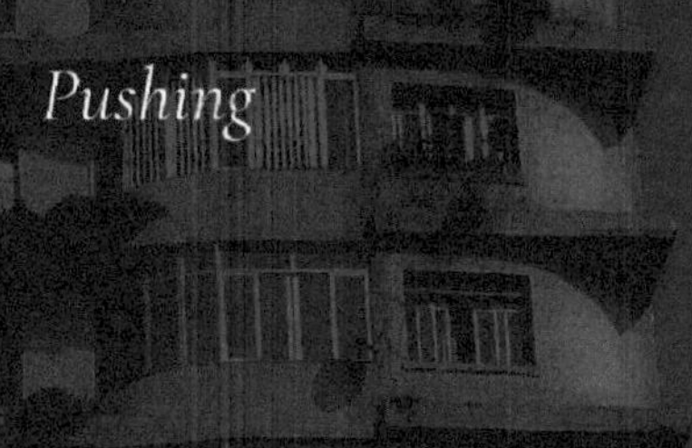

Riding Blind Intentions

I'm stuck in a phase,
Might as well be a maze.
I'm lapped by each day,
They all feel the same.
I'm cloudy.
Hazy at best,
Down but who's counting?
No rest makes me lazy,
No smile, no frowning
Head down,
Feet on the ground pounding,
Keep on keeping on,
Pay no mind when I'm doubting.

Make Things

You're low,
No need be hopeless.
Stay seeking progress.
The process a slow bitch
So know it ain't growthless.
In the bed of my choosing,
Ain't much but it suits me.
Not tryna being flashy,
My own manufactured.
Built slow and it's lasting,
Not much but I have it.

Via Negativa

The world keeps on turning,
Bet house it's a sure thing,
You learn the whole journey,
Get stripes when you earn them.
Life will keep toying,
It's lived best enjoying.
No expectations
So plans never foiled.
If I try and fail
I could die in peace.
Let my greed prevail,
I couldn't rest easy.
Avoiding regrets,
Take a breath and reflect,
Make the most of my chances,
How many I'll get?
Life is a canvas,
I paint in abstractions
It's nothing fantastic
But soothes me like magic.

Antifragile

Take the beating, I need it.
I'm fiending to feel it.
Beats numbness, I mean it.
Grit teeth the pain frees me.
When I'm writhing and reeling
I block out the feelings,
Think only on real things,
The while repeating -
Come along, the night is gone.
The day has come, the sun is up.
You've got the strength so strap in, harness.
Reach deep, tap in, wait out the darkness.

Dawn

Come along,
The night is gone.
The day has come,
The sun is up.
You've got the strength, so
Strap in, harness.
Reach deep, tap in,
Wait out the darkness.

Quality Quest

We've all got the power
To grow up and think,
Sprout like a flower
Unique like the ink
That carries the thoughts
From my brain to the page
But they're worth nothing at all
Like a seed in the dark
Where the growth never starts.
I know I can't help
But I feel it's my fault.
All by myself,
There's no need to talk,
Cognitive space
To jot down these bars.
I'll barter my time like a martyr.
Not the answer
But it's better than nada.
Damn sure not smarter
So I gotta try harder.
I'll be honest,
I'm not flawless.
I know where I strong
And I know where I'm weak.
For the truths that I seek.

Pushing

Uncovered flaws
Leave me jarred
But at least I can sleep.
I'll keep trekking farther,
Don't bother
The pain in my feet.
The rain and the sleet
Don't keep my fire from burning.
My irises burning,
I'm thirsty,
No Visine, I'm hurting.
I don't care if its working,
I've decided for certain.
If there's a lord hear my purpose,
For sure it ain't worthless.
I'll take all your curses
To pass on my message.
Up to them to have read it,
Did my part when I sent it.
Good thing my heart isn't hesitant,
Not done, no relenting.
If I said it I meant it,
Thought it all the way through.
I've been in a groove,
Still got my youth
But feel older.
I'm holding a candle to it,
I'm a soldier.

Reading Into Randomness

Look at this, it's been a bit,
So far shit hasn't fell through.
Let's wing it, call it red bull,
Been a minute since I let loose.
I've been through shit but I'll admit
Them failures barely helpful.
These night sweats can get dreadful,
I just can't slow my tempo.
All wheel drive, this bumpy road,
I'm antifragile, overload me.
Steady progress, I don't know
What I'm approaching, One day hopefully.
I've set my sights so I'm alright
To wait and not be knowing.
I've been out here like a lone wolf.
I'm afraid I'll just keep going.

Signal-Searching In Noise

I'm too into the moment,
Sometimes it feels like coasting.
I've been going with the flow now
For so long, it's all I'm knowing.
I've been crashing like an ocean,
Now I'm floating, searching, hoping.
Head down pressing forward,
Just keep going, just keep going.

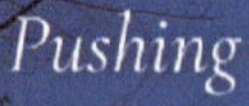

Individuation

I'll go my way,
Keep these feet on this pavement.
Farewell, namaste,
Bon voyage, go on safely.
I've been on this road,
Through the sun and the snow
And I keep pressing forward,
All I know is keep going.

Even If

What in the fuck
Did I just wake up from?
My eyes are all crusty,
Vision is double,
Quick, let me recover.
Oh brother, this dream,
It's inside another.
I might just go deeper,
I'm already under.
I'd be underachieving,
Even if my demons took cover.

Homeostasis

I'm tired of riding
This damn roller coaster.
I'm high for the highs
Then the lows leave me sober.
I know I'd break even,
Even if my demons took over.

Failure As Feedback

I've died inside
A million times,
Not a peep but
I feel like screaming.
Won't give in so
Long as I'm breathing,
Even if my
Demons have leevrage.

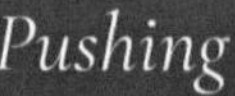

Mustering Intertia

What in the fuck
Could I say that's worth hearing?
There's slack in these sails
Since I don't feel like steering.
I'm facing my fears
But they slow me down clearly.

Manic Hyperphantasia

A million tries
To get it right,
What the fuck is a million more?
These swirling skies,
It's time to rise,
I've enjoyed the eye of the storm.
My feet are fine,
It's my will that's sore.
Don't need a ride,
I've set my course.
I'm here all the same,
If it rains let it pour on.
I'll die on my sword,
For now take my word for it.

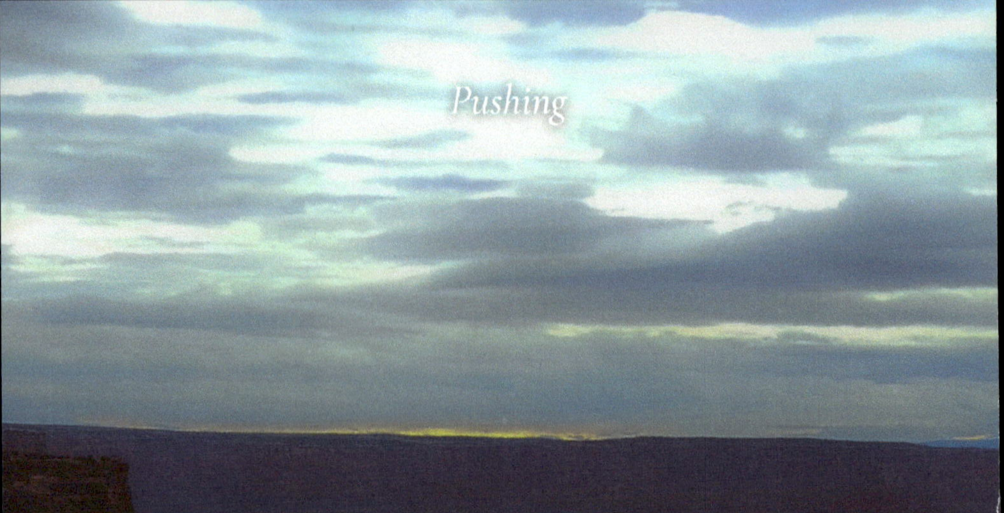

Entropy Oriented

There's something 'bout stumbling
And grunting for nothing.
I'm up against the wall
But I ain't yet done bumped it.
This road gon' be bumpy,
I'm ready to rough it.
I'm stuck in discomfort,
Convinced that my love hurts.

Pushing

Reconciling the Road

How in the fuck did I get here?
Where did I think I was going?
I signed up for tough sledding,
Rough stretches still get me.
I carry the load but
I ain't learned my lessons.

Bayesian Reset

I underestimated
How far I would make it.
There's more for the taking
Unless I'm lost chasing.
My demons go hide
When they know that I'll face them.
A million more tries
Even if I lose patience.

..and much thanks to
my loved ones

www.ingramcontent.com/pod-product-compliance
Lightning Source LLC
LaVergne TN
LVHW052305100826
845147LV00006B/679

* 9 7 9 8 2 1 8 7 0 4 2 0 9 *